D1159138

ALL AROUND THE WORLD
HAITI

by Clara Bennington

Ideas for Parents and Teachers

Pogo Books let children practice reading informational text while introducing them to nonfiction features such as headings, labels, sidebars, maps, and diagrams, as well as a table of contents, glossary, and index.

Carefully leveled text with a strong photo match offers early fluent readers the support they need to succeed.

Before Reading

- "Walk" through the book and point out the various nonfiction features. Ask the student what purpose each feature serves.
- Look at the glossary together. Read and discuss the words.

Read the Book

- Have the child read the book independently.
- Invite him or her to list questions that arise from reading.

After Reading

- Discuss the child's questions. Talk about how he or she might find answers to those questions.
- Prompt the child to think more. Ask: Haiti has struggled partly because of some of the leaders in charge. What do you think the qualities of a good leader are?

Pogo Books are published by Jump!
5357 Penn Avenue South
Minneapolis, MN 55419
www.jumplibrary.com

Copyright © 2019 Jump!
International copyright reserved in all countries.
No part of this book may be reproduced in any form without written permission from the publisher.

Library of Congress Cataloging-in-Publication Data

Names: Bennington, Clara, author.
Title: Haiti / by Clara Bennington.
Description: Minneapolis, MN : Jump!, Inc., 2018.
Series: All Around the World | "Pogo Books."
Includes bibliographical references and index.
Identifiers: LCCN 2018004331 (print)
LCCN 2018003800 (ebook) | ISBN 9781641281270 (ebook)
ISBN 9781641281256 (hardcover : alk. paper)
ISBN 9781641281263 (pbk.)
Subjects: LCSH: Haiti—Juvenile literature.
Classification: LCC F1915.2 (print) | LCC F1915.2 .B46 2019 (ebook) | DDC 972.94—dc23
LC record available at https://lccn.loc.gov/2018004331

Editor: Kristine Spanier
Book Designer: Leah Sanders

Photo Credits: tropicalpixsingapore/iStock, cover; Jose Nicolas/Getty, 1; Pixfiction/Shutterstock, 3; John Seaton Callahan/Getty, 4, 5; montree imnam/Shutterstock, 6; Erika Santelices/Getty, 6–7; margo1778/Shutterstock, 8–9; colaimages/Alamy, 10 (frame); windu/Shutterstock, 10 (background); The Photolibrary Wales/Alamy, 11; Bart Pro/Alamy, 12–13; Thony Belizaire/Getty, 14–15; Anne-Marie Weber/Getty, 16–17; Golden Richard/Alamy, 18; Hector Retamal/Getty, 19; Reynold Mainse/Getty, 20–21; arindambanerjee/Shutterstock, 23.

Printed in the United States of America at Corporate Graphics in North Mankato, Minnesota.

TABLE OF CONTENTS

CHAPTER 1

WELCOME TO HAITI!

Alo! That is how you say "hello" in Haiti. This country is located on a large island in the Caribbean Sea.

The country has high mountains and hills. Rivers flow through the land. Golden beaches line the coast. Clear blue water fills the seas. Let's learn about this interesting country!

The country shares a border with the Dominican Republic. Many Haitians work on that country's **plantations**. Some students attend college there. The two countries trade **goods**.

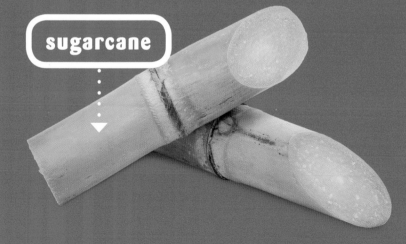

sugarcane

sugarcane

mangoes ·····▶

It is warm and humid here. Spring and fall are the rainy seasons. **Hurricanes** often happen from June through November.

The **climate** is good for growing **crops**. What grows here? Coffee. Mangoes. Cocoa. Sugarcane. Rice. Corn. Wood.

CHAPTER 2

A COUNTRY'S STRUGGLES

In 1957, a **dictator** became president. His name was François Duvalier. He did not treat the people well. When he died in 1971, his son took his place. He was also unfair. He was forced to leave in 1986.

François Duvalier

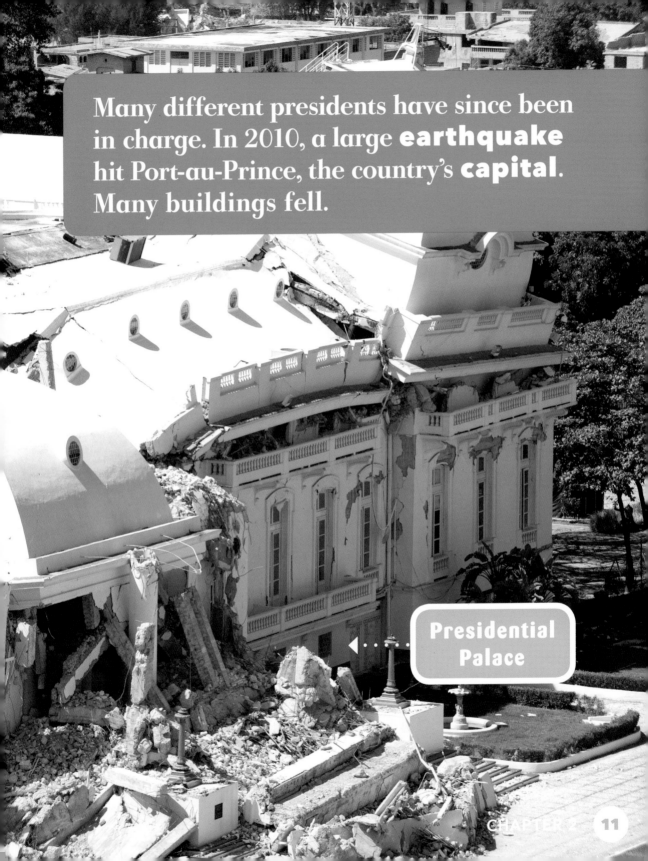

Many different presidents have since been in charge. In 2010, a large **earthquake** hit Port-au-Prince, the country's **capital**. Many buildings fell.

Presidential Palace

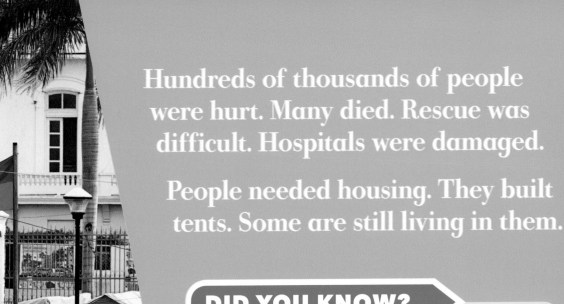

Hundreds of thousands of people were hurt. Many died. Rescue was difficult. Hospitals were damaged.

People needed housing. They built tents. Some are still living in them.

DID YOU KNOW?

Many countries wanted to help after the earthquake. Healthcare workers and engineers arrived. Billions of dollars in **aid** were sent.

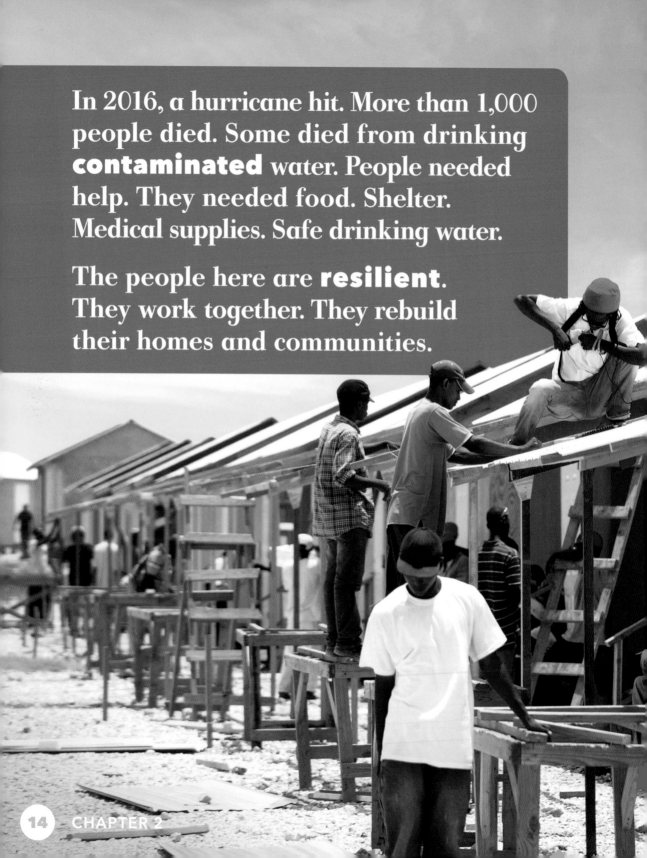

In 2016, a hurricane hit. More than 1,000 people died. Some died from drinking **contaminated** water. People needed help. They needed food. Shelter. Medical supplies. Safe drinking water.

The people here are **resilient**. They work together. They rebuild their homes and communities.

TAKE A LOOK!

The picture in the country's flag is meaningful to the citizens. Each element symbolizes an important value. The **motto** is in French. It means, "Union Makes Strength."

FREEDOM

INDEPENDENCE

L'UNION FAIT LA FORCE

DEFENSE OF FREEDOM

ENDING OF SLAVERY

More than half of the people here live in **poverty**. Why? Many depend on farming for income. **Natural disasters** destroy the crops. Low levels of education contribute to poverty. So does the **unstable** government.

CHAPTER 3

CREATIVE CITIZENS

People here like to listen to music. They tell stories. Sometimes they act them out with songs and dances.

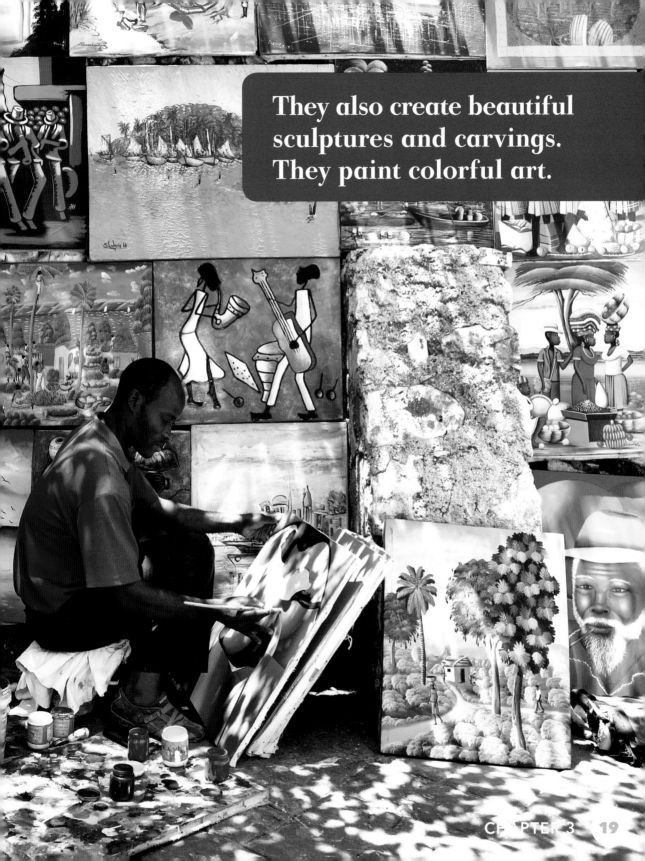

They also create beautiful sculptures and carvings. They paint colorful art.

Meals are made with food from the island. The people enjoy beans, rice, corn, and yams. Their food is flavored with garlic and hot peppers. On January 1, Independence Day is celebrated with pumpkin soup. Fudge and doughnuts are popular treats.

There is a lot to learn about this country. Would you like to visit?

QUICK FACTS & TOOLS

HAITI

Location: Caribbean Sea

Size: 10,714 square miles
(27,750 square kilometers)

Population: 10,646,714
(July 2017 estimate)

Capital: Port-au-Prince

Type of Government:
semi-presidential republic

Languages: French and Creole

Exports: clothing, oils, cocoa,
mangoes, coffee

GLOSSARY

aid: Money or equipment for people in need.

capital: A city where government leaders meet.

climate: The weather typical of a certain place over a long period of time.

colonists: People who leave one area to settle another.

contaminated: Containing harmful substances.

crops: Plants grown for food.

dictator: A ruler who has complete control of a country, often by force.

earthquake: A sudden, violent shaking of Earth that may damage buildings and cause injuries.

goods: Things that are traded or sold.

hurricanes: Violent storms with heavy rain and high winds.

independence: Freedom from a controlling authority.

motto: A short phrase that states a belief.

natural disasters: Natural events such as floods, earthquakes, or hurricanes that cause great damage or loss of life.

plantations: Large farms found in warm climates.

poverty: The state of being poor.

resilient: Capable of recovering from misfortune or change.

unstable: Likely to change.

INDEX

TO LEARN MORE

Learning more is as easy as 1, 2, 3.

1) Go to www.factsurfer.com

2) Enter "Haiti" into the search box.

3) Click the "Surf" button to see a list of websites.

With factsurfer, finding more information is just a click away.